The ABRSM **SONGBOOK**

Book 1

ABRSM

Compiled by Ross Campbell, Robert Forbes and Lilija Zobens

Published by ABRSM (Publishing) Ltd, a wholly owned subsidiary of ABRSM

© 2008 by The Associated Board of the Royal Schools of Music

Reprinted in 2009, 2010, 2011, 2012, 2013, 2015, 2016, 2018

ISBN 978 1 86096 597 5

AB 3128

Music origination by Barnes Music Engraving Ltd
Cover and text design by Vermillion
Printed in England by Halstan & Co. Ltd, Amersham, Bucks.,
on materials from sustainable sources

Contents

Singers using these books to prepare for ABRSM graded Singing exams are encouraged to check the current syllabus for full details of requirements before making their choices.

Introduction

The ABRSM Songbook series includes five progressively graded anthologies of song repertoire for teachers and singers of all ages and voice types.

Encompassing a wide range of periods, genres, themes and moods, the series is designed to provide musical interest and technical challenge over many years of vocal study, suggest varied choices for recital programming, and make available selected repertoire for those preparing for ABRSM graded Singing exams. As well as including over 100 art songs of the highest quality (many in new arrangements or editions), the series also contains a truly international collection of 60 unaccompanied traditional songs representing 26 different countries.

Every piece has been expertly researched and is presented here in clear new engraving. Song texts are always given both in their original language and with an English-language singing translation (many of which were specially commissioned for the series). Some of the songs have been transposed from their original keys to ensure that they can be sung by as wide a range of voice types as possible. For all songs, helpful background notes have been included. The collections are topped off with a CD containing 'minus-one' piano recordings of the art song accompaniments, in addition to spoken pronunciation guides for every original text, narrated by native speakers. CD track numbers are given within ◐ before each piece. We hope that these useful extra features will help singers and teachers with the study and performance of this wealth of wonderful songs.

Biographies

Ross Campbell is Professor of Singing at the Royal Academy of Music, London, and Head of Singing and Music at Guildford School of Acting.

Robert Forbes was formerly Head of Singing at the Birmingham School of Speech and Drama, and is currently Singing Tutor at the Guildford School of Acting.

Lilija Zobens is a singing teacher in Enfield and Hertfordshire schools. She studied folklore with the singer and collector A. L. (Bert) Lloyd and has researched and performed songs of the Balkans and her native Latvia.

Carol Barratt is a composer and leading music educationalist. Her compositions range from works for young children to concert repertoire.

Art Songs

Compiled by Ross Campbell
and Robert Forbes

Compilers' note

It was a rare opportunity and privilege to play, sing through and analyse every song that appears in the ABRSM syllabus for Grade 1. The experience revealed the wide range of song repertoire covered by the syllabus lists. It was therefore not an easy task to select which of the many fine songs should be included in this songbook, so it is important to explain the criteria which affected our choices.

The foremost thought in our minds was how the structure of the exam should inform the early stages of programme planning for a recital; our choices were made in order to present a range of styles and periods, with differing moods and pace, to encourage an interesting and varied exam programme – of the sort that is also expected in a recital. We also considered that the songbook choices should present a variety of technical demands appropriate to the grade, be accessible to all voice types, and be suitable for as wide an age range as possible. Finally, we chose some songs which are not often performed, but which, because of their quality, deserve to be brought before a wider audience.

However, it needs to be said that this songbook is a valuable tool for both teacher and singer irrespective of whether an exam is to be undertaken. By presenting a selection of songs from the folk, classical, musical theatre and light music styles, this songbook should be a benchmark to which the singer can aspire, as well as a rich source of vocal repertoire.

Ross Campbell and Robert Forbes

Notes on the editorial approach

Most public domain works have been re-edited from contemporary sources. Key signatures and time signatures have been modernized. Tempo marks have been supplied where the original has none, also a few additional dynamics; details of research and editorial changes can be found in the 'Notes on the art songs' (pp. 6–9), though obvious errors have been corrected without comment. All metronome marks in square brackets are editorial. Melismatic slurs have been provided for the vocal line without comment, whether or not they occur in the source. Beaming of the vocal part has also been modernized. Where songs have been transposed from the original, the figured bass has been modified to fit the new key. Suggestions for ornamentation have been given above the stave where appropriate, but it is hoped that singers will be encouraged to invent their own.

As far as possible, early published sources have been used for the melodies of folksongs.

I must thank the librarians of the British Library and the Royal College of Music for their help; also Kathleen Bentley for finding sources of the French folksongs, Dr Rhian Davies for checking the texts of the Welsh folksongs, Lada Valesova for help with Czech text, and Jose Luis Rodriguez for information on 'La Cucaracha'.

Michael Pilkington

Notes by (in alphabetical order) Anthony Burton, Ross Campbell and Robert Forbes, with contributions from Michael Pilkington

Notes on the art songs

A dream is a wish your heart makes

The rags-to-riches fairy story of Cinderella, first written down in the 1st century B. C. E., has been retold with music in many operas, ballets and pantomimes, and in films including Walt Disney's popular animated version of 1950. This has songs by Mack David (1912–93), Al Hoffman (1902–60) and Jerry Livingston (1909–87) – including 'A dream is a wish your heart makes', sung by Cinderella to encourage her animal friends. (The instruction 'tacet' in the piano part in b. 24 applies to the three right-hand notes in that bar doubling the melody, but it is optional.)

Auprès de ma blonde

'Auprès de ma blonde', sometimes called 'Le prisonnier de Hollande' or 'The Prisoner of Holland', is a French folksong dating from the European wars of the 17th century. It has often been sung by troops on the march, for example by French-Canadian soldiers during the First World War. This version of the tune and the French words is taken from a 1984 anthology, *Le Livre des Chansons de France*. Notice that all the phrases in bb. 1–12 begin with an up-beat, whereas those of the refrain begin on the down-beat, giving them a different character. The accompaniment is newly composed; Carol Barratt suggests that if it is played on a digital piano the 'harpsichord' voice might be suitable.

Cuckoo

Martin Shaw (1875–1958) studied at the Royal College of Music with Charles Villiers Stanford, and worked in London in the theatre and as a church organist. He is probably best remembered as compiler, with Percy Dearmer and Ralph Vaughan Williams, of the hymn book *Songs of Praise* and the *Oxford Book of Carols*. His compositions include music for parish worship and over 100 songs. 'Cuckoo', a setting of a traditional first verse with an anonymously added second, was published in 1915. Each verse begins with the bird's well-known two-note call, in the piano part as well as the voice.

Die Nachtigall

Johannes Brahms (1833–97) was one of the great composers of his age, a master of every form of concert music. The long list of his songs includes two sets of arrangements of German folksongs, and a further set of *Volks-Kinderlieder*, 'Folksongs for children', arranged in 1857 and published the following year by J. Rieter-Biedermann with a dedication to the children of Brahms's friends Robert and Clara Schumann. The second of these is 'Die Nachtigall', a charming setting of a folksong with dialect words. The acciaccaturas in bb. 8 and 11, suggesting the fluttering of the nightingale, should be sung as quickly as possible and on the beat.

Dona, dona

'Dona, dona' is a well-known song in Yiddish, the language (related to German) used for centuries in Jewish communities in central and eastern Europe, and subsequently all over the world. The song was written for a production of a play called *Esterke un Kazimir der groyser*, about the 14th-century Polish King Casimir the Great and his Jewish concubine Esther, at the Yiddish Art Theatre in New York in 1940. The words are by the author of the play, Aaron Zeitlin (1889–1973), and the music by the Ukrainian-American composer Sholom Secunda (1894–1974); the standard English translation is by Arthur Kevess and the singer Teddi Schwartz. The Aeolian mode of the melody, with minor 3rd and 6th and a flattened 7th, reflects the melancholy plight of the calf tied up to be carried to market – probably, given the date of the song, an allusion to the plight of European Jews under the Nazi regime.

Good morrow to you, springtime!

The Scottish musician Sir Hugh (Stevenson) Roberton (1874–1952) was the founding conductor of the Glasgow Orpheus Choir, which made several much-loved recordings, and he composed numerous songs for choirs and solo voices. 'Good morrow to you, springtime!', a setting of words by P. A. Grand for (originally) unison voices, was published in 1947. Observing the various *ritardando* (*rit*) markings subtly and without exaggeration will help to produce the 'touch of coyness' asked for in the tempo direction.

Grandfather Clock

Thomas Dunhill (1877–1946) taught at Eton College and at the Royal College of Music in London, was an examiner for the Associated Board, wrote several books on music, and composed light operas, ballets, orchestral, chamber and instrumental music, and many songs. Some of the songs are settings of poems by Margaret Rose, whose words were also set by other British composers including Michael Head, Armstrong Gibbs and John Longmire. The witty 'Grandfather Clock' was published, as a song for unison singing, after Dunhill's death.

Home on the Range

The words of 'Home on the Range' were written in 1872 by Dr Brewster Higley (1822–1911), and first set to music by Daniel E. Kelley. The song was popular all over the southwestern United States through the 1880s and 1890s. During this time the words were modified, and a new tune created, a version of which was published in 1905. The words were then attributed to Mrs W. M. Goodwin and the tune, similar to the current one, to William Goodwin. However, it was proved in 1935 that this version of both words and tune existed as early as 1874. 'Home on the Range' is now the state song of Kansas, and has taken on the status, and the multiple variants, of a folksong. The version of words and melody here is taken from *Cowboy Songs and other Frontier Ballads* by the father-and-son song collectors John and Alan Lomax. This source gives Dan Kelley's quite different original tune as an alternative version.

La Cucaracha

'La Cucaracha' is the Spanish word for a cockroach, though it has many other slang meanings. It is the title of a well-known traditional Mexican dance song which may well have its origins in the Renaissance, but which reached its greatest popularity during the Mexican Revolution of 1910. Verses were often improvised, and there are many different printed versions of the text; those in this volume are newly written. The melody here is taken from Carl Sandburg's 1927 anthology *The American Songbag*, in which it is credited as having been collected by F. S. Curtis of the Texas Folk Lore Society. The accompaniment brings out the implied cross-rhythms of 6/8 against 3/4 in the refrain. Before the refrain, the accompanist should leave the singer room for a quickly snatched breath.

Noël nouvelet

'Noël nouvelet' is a traditional French noël or carol, intended to be sung at New Year rather than Christmas, which is well known in numerous choral arrangements. The earliest appearance of its text is in a manuscript of the late 15th century. The melody (in the Dorian mode, with minor 3rd and major 6th) has been associated with the words at least since the 17th century; it may indeed be the original tune. The version of the text and melody given here was collected by Léon Roques in the 19th century, and printed in a volume of French folksongs for children in 1936. The phrases need to be shaped differently according to whether you are singing in French or English.

Omens of Spring

W. H. (William Henry) Anderson (1882–1955) was an English tenor and composer who emigrated to Canada in 1910 for the sake of his health. He settled in Winnipeg, Manitoba, where he became well known as a singing teacher, composer and arranger of songs and choral music, and choral conductor; he directed a regular series of choral broadcasts on national radio for nearly thirty years. This song, originally intended for unison voices, is the second number in a posthumously published sequence called *Omens of Spring*, with words by an unknown poet. It requires clear enunciation of the text within a smooth melodic line; notice the dotted rhythms in bb. 13 and 15.

Quem pastores laudavere

'Quem pastores laudavere' is a Christmas hymn with Latin words from 14th- or early 15th-century Germany. In later centuries it was often performed during Lutheran Christmas Eve services, divided up among soloists or choirs in several high galleries to suggest a circling choir of angels. This edition presents the hymn in a four-part harmonization by Johann Hermann Schein (1586–1630), a predecessor of J. S. Bach as Cantor of St Thomas's, Leipzig, as he published it in his *Cantional* in 1627. The rhythm has been slightly modernized but the harmony follows the source.

Source: second edition, *Cantional, oder Gesang-Buch Augspurgische Confession* (Leipzig, 1645)

Song of the Boats

Betty Roe was born in 1930 in London, studied piano, cello, singing and composition at the Royal Academy of Music, and was later a church organist and conductor, a pop music session singer, and for ten years director of music at the London Academy of Music and Dramatic Art. The long list of her compositions includes church music, musicals and many songs. Roe's *Ten Ponder and William Songs*, published in 1987 for voice or unison voices and piano, have texts from Barbara Softly's children's book about a small boy called William and his friend Ponder, a pyjama-case who makes up songs for him. The second, 'Song of the Boats', has the sturdy character of a sea shanty, almost with two beats to the bar rather than four.

The Crocodile

Peter Jenkyns (1921–96) was a schoolteacher in Hertfordshire, a singer and musical director, and composer of several works for the harmonica as well as a good deal of educational music. His humorous 'The Crocodile', originally written as a unison song, was published in 1962. In the last verse (b. 39), the direction *ad lib.* means that the singer should sing more freely as well as slower (the instruction *colla voce*, or 'with the voice', in the piano part tells the accompanist to follow) – but the ending is at *Tempo I*.

The Miller of Dee

'The Miller of Dee' is a folksong: the river Dee in question is presumably the one that rises in the Welsh mountains and reaches the sea near the English city of Chester. The melody has a Welsh flavour, with a minor-key melancholy somewhat at odds with the supposedly 'jolly' character of the self-reliant miller. The first verse appeared with a very similar tune in *Love in a Village* (1762), a 'pasticcio' compiled by the writer Isaac Bickerstaff and the composer Thomas Arne which combined folksongs with Italian arias and newly written numbers. The words and melody of this version are taken from a collection published in London in 1782 under the title of *The Convivial Songster*.

The Spinning Wheel

'The Spinning Wheel' is a traditional Irish tune, with words written to fit it by the Irish poet John Francis Waller (1810–94). The accompaniment provided in this arrangement suggests the regular movement of the spinning wheel, and implies equally smooth delivery of the vocal line. The melody is reproduced from the 1992 anthology *Songs of Ireland*, the text from *A Victorian Anthology*, published in the USA in 1896. In the original poem, the chorus comes after every two verses, not every verse. In verse 2, 'achora' (b. 3) means 'my love'.

Walking in the Air

The British composer Howard Blake (born 1938) has written concert music for orchestras, choirs and many different ensembles. But by far his best known piece is *The Snowman*, based on the cartoon book of the same name by Raymond Briggs. In 1982 he wrote the words and music for an animated television version which has become a perennial Christmas favourite; and since then he has adapted his score as a concert piece with narrator, a ballet and a full-length stage show. At the heart of *The Snowman* in all its versions is the song sung by the young hero as he is taken off by a snowman to the North Pole, and finds himself 'Walking in the Air'. Notice the contrast between the haunting main melody, in the Aeolian mode, and bb. 28–35 and 53–61 with their less stable harmony, different rhythmic accentuation and curving four-bar phrases.

Where is love?

Lionel Bart (1930–99) was a British songwriter and composer of musicals. He had his greatest success with *Oliver!*, based on Charles Dickens's novel *Oliver Twist*, for which he wrote both music and lyrics. It was staged in London in 1960 and in New York in 1963, and in 1968 was made into an Oscar-winning film. The central figure, Oliver Twist, is a young orphan who is sent to the workhouse and later falls among thieves. In Act I, he is apprenticed to an undertaker and sent to sleep among the coffins: in his dejection he sings the touching song 'Where is love?'

Disc 1

(1) Piano accompaniment

(2) Pronunciation guide

A dream is a wish your heart makes

from Cinderella

Words and music by
Mack David (1912–93), Al Hoffman (1902–60)
and Jerry Livingston (1909–87)

Disc 1

③ Piano accompaniment

④ Pronunciation guide

Auprès de ma blonde

So near to my blond girl

English words by
Elizabeth Eva Leach

French traditional

arr. Carol Barratt

AB 3128

CHORUS

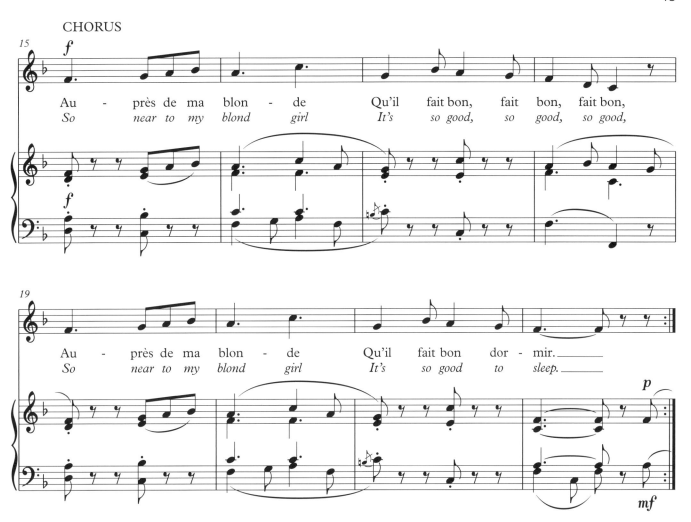

Au - près de ma blon - de Qu'il fait bon, fait bon, fait bon,
So near to my blond girl It's so good, so good, so good,

Au - près de ma blon - de Qu'il fait bon dor - mir.
So near to my blond girl It's so good to sleep.

3. Ell' chante pour les filles
   Qui n'ont pas de mari.
   Pour moi ne chante guère
   Car j'en ai un joli.
   Auprès de ma blonde…

4. 'Mais dites-moi donc belle
   Où est votre mari?'
   'Il est dans la Hollande,
   Les Hollandais l'ont pris!'
   Auprès de ma blonde…

5. 'Que donneriez vous, belle,
   A qui l'ira quéri?'
   'Je donnerais Touraine,
   Paris et Saint-Denis,
   Auprès de ma blonde…

6. Les tours de Notre-Dame,
   Le clocher de mon pays.
   Et ma joli' colombe
   Qui chante jour et nuit.'
   *Auprès de ma blonde…

3. *It sings for all the daughters
   Who have not yet been wed.
   It hardly sings for me though
   For I've my handsome Ned.
   So near to my blond girl…*

4. *'But tell me then my lovely
   Where is your man today?'
   'He's been detained in Holland,
   The Dutch took him away!'
   So near to my blond girl…*

5. *'What would you give to him, dear,
   Who seeks your man afar?'
   'Oh, Saint Denis and Paris,
   The valley of the Loire,
   So near to my blond girl…*

6. *The towers of Notre-Dame, too,
   The town clock of Marseille.
   And my delightful sparrow
   That sings both night and day.'
   So near to my blond girl…

* For the accompaniment to the final chorus, turn to the next page.

CODA (last chorus)

Au - près de ma blon - de Qu'il fait bon, fait bon, fait bon,
So near to my blond girl It's so good, so good, so good,

Au - près de ma blon - de Qu'il fait bon dor - mir.
So near to my blond girl It's so good to sleep.

accel. al fine

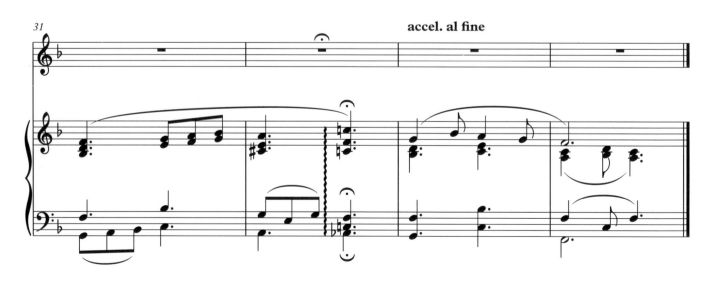

Disc 1

⑤ Piano accompaniment

⑥ Pronunciation guide

to Percy Dearmer

Cuckoo

Martin Shaw
(1875–1958)

Far a-way O-ver the sea To Spain___ I fly a-gain;

Day and night I take my flight.

Cuck - oo, Good - bye_____ to

poco rit.

you.

pp

Disc 1

⑨ Piano accompaniment
⑩ Pronunciation guide

Dona, dona

Aaron Zeitlin
(1889–1973)

English words by Sheldon Secunda, Arthur Kevess
and Teddi Schwartz

Sholom Sholem Secunda
(1894–1974)

arr. Carol Barratt

Fondly [♩ = *c*.100]

1. Oy - fn furl___ ligt dos kel - bl, ligt ge - bun - dn___ mit a shtrik.
On a wa - gon bound for mar - ket, There's a calf with a mourn - ful eye.

2. Shrayt dos kel - bl, zogt der poy - er: ver zhe heyst dikh___ zayn a kalb?
'Stop com - plain - ing!' said the far - mer. 'Who told you a___ calf to be?

3. Bid - ne kel - ber tut men bin - dn un men shlept zey___ un men shekht,
Calves are ea - si - ly bound and slaugh - tered, Nev - er know - ing the rea - son why,

Hoykh in hi - ml flit dos shvel - bl, freyt zikh, dreyt zikh___ hin un krik.
High a - bove him, there's a swal - low, Wing - ing swift - ly___ through the sky.

Volst ge - kert tsu zayn a foy - gl, volst ge - kert tsu___ zayn a shvalb.
Why don't you have wings to fly___ with Like the swal - low,___ proud and free?'

ver s'hot fli - gl, flit a - royft - su, iz bay key - nem___ nit keyn knekht.
But who - ev - er trea - sures free - dom Like the swal - low will learn to fly.

Disc 1

11 Piano accompaniment

12 Pronunciation guide

to Wendy

Good morrow to you, springtime!

P. A. Grand

Hugh S. Roberton
(1874–1952)

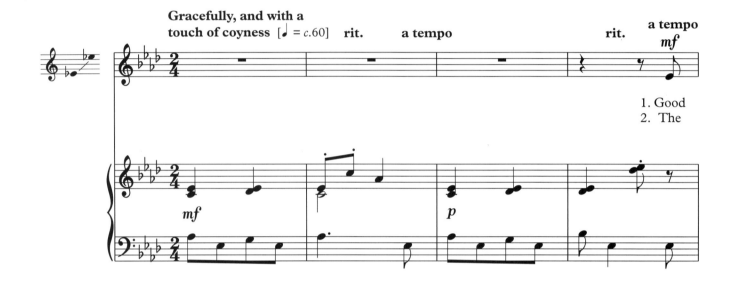

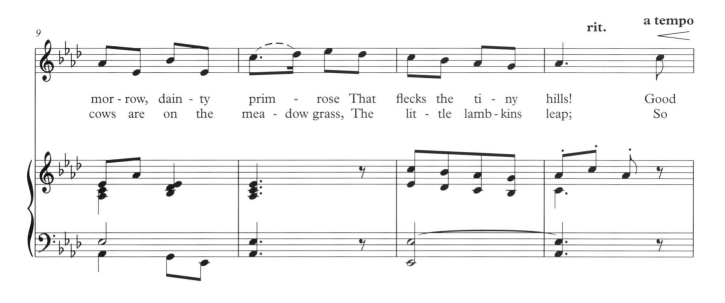

rit.　a tempo

mor - row, dain - ty prim - rose That flecks the ti - ny hills! Good
cows are on the mea - dow grass, The lit - tle lamb - kins leap; So

rit.　a tempo

mor - row pret - ty cuck - oo That sings in yon - der tree: The
wake, you love - ly cel - an - dine, You cro - cus, smile, for see At

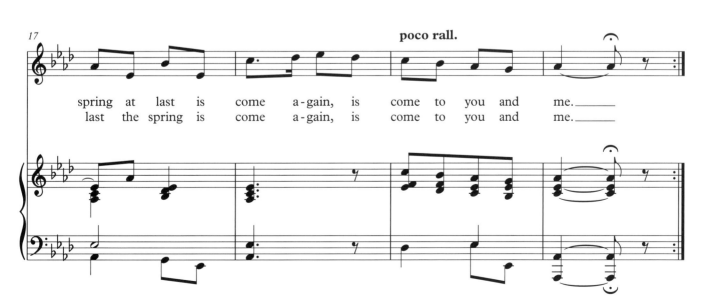

poco rall.

spring at last is come a - gain, is come to you and me.____
last the spring is come a - gain, is come to you and me.____

Disc 1

(13) Piano accompaniment

(14) Pronunciation guide

Grandfather Clock

Margaret Rose

Thomas F. Dunhill
(1877–1946)

Strictly in time, like a ticking clock [♩. = c.84]

Tick - tock! Grand-fa-ther Clock, What do you do all

day?____ I tick the min-utes, and one by one I tick the hours a - way.

Tick - tock! Grand-fa-ther Clock, What do you do all night?___ My bus - y wheels must go

Disc 1

(15) Piano accompaniment

(17) Pronunciation guide

Home on the Range

Dr Brewster Higley
(1822–1911)

American traditional
arr. Carol Barratt

3. How often at night when the heavens are bright
With the light of the glittering stars,
Have I stood here amazed and asked as I gazed
If their glory exceeds that of ours.
Home, home on the range,…

4. Oh, I love these wild flowers in this dear land of ours;
The curlew I love to hear scream;
And I love the white rocks and the antelope flocks
That graze on the mountain-tops green.
Home, home on the range,…

5. Oh, give me a land where the bright diamond sand
Flows leisurely down the stream;
Where the graceful white swan goes gliding along
Like a maid in a heavenly dream.
Home, home on the range,…

* 6. Then I would not exchange my home on the range,
Where the deer and the antelope play;
Where seldom is heard a discouraging word
And the skies are not cloudy all day.
Home, home on the range,…

* For the accompaniment to this verse (or whichever verse is performed as the final verse) turn to the next page.

Disc 1

16 Piano accompaniment

17 Pronunciation guide

Home on the Range

Dr Brewster Higley
(1822–1911)

American traditional
arr. Alan Bullard

word And the skies are not clou - dy all day.

gazed If their glo - ry ex - ceeds that of ours.

- long Like a maid in a hea - ven-ly dream.

CHORUS

Home, home on the range, Where the deer and the

an - te - lope play; Where sel - dom is heard a dis -

- cou - ra - ging word And the skies are not clou - dy all day.

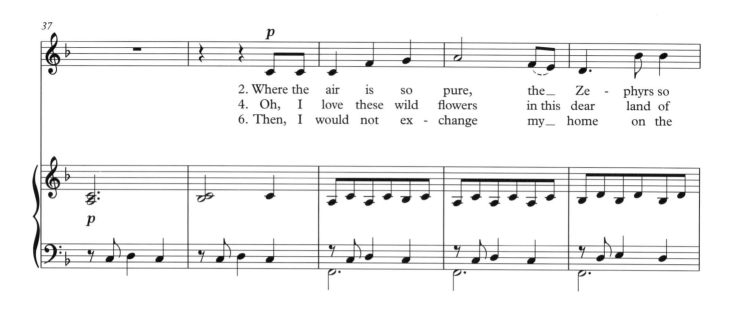

2. Where the air is so pure, the Ze - phyrs so
4. Oh, I love these wild flowers in this dear land of
6. Then, I would not ex - change my home on the

free, The breez - es so bal - my and light,_____ That I
ours; The cur - lew I love to hear scream;_____ And I
range, Where the deer and the an - te-lope play;_____ Where

would not ex - change my home on the range For all of the
love the white rocks and the an - te-lope flocks That graze on the
sel - dom is heard a dis - cou - ra-ging word And the skies are not

Disc 1
18 Piano accompaniment
19 Pronunciation guide

La Cucaracha

Robin Barry
(born 1972)

Mexican traditional
arr. Carol Barratt

1. Come the dawn of the Fi - es - ta, Ear - ly morn - ing sun is creep - ing
2. Red, and white, and green the ban - ners, Bright bal - loons and stream - ers flutt - 'ring,
3. At the stalls a - round the pla - za Smell the en - chi - la - das cook - ing,
4. Sound your trum - pets, toot your whis - tles, Hear the loud ma - ra - cas shak - ing,
5. Señ - o - ri - tas, ca - bal - le - ros, Come and dance with one an - o - ther:

Through the cracks in doors and shut - ters, Wak - ing all the chil - dren sleep - ing.
Fill - ing all the town with col - ours, Sway - ing gai - ly from the gutt - 'ring.
Gua - ca - mo - le, hot tor - til - las, Eat your fill, there's no - one look - ing!
Bark - ing mad - ly those chi - hua - huas What a joy - ful noise they're mak - ing!
Some be - lieve 'La Cu - ca - ra - cha' Finds a girl or boy their lov - er!

* This accompaniment can be used for whichever verse is performed as the final verse.

Disc 1
(20) Piano accompaniment
(21) Pronunciation guide

Noël nouvelet

Sing now Christ is born

English words by
Elizabeth Eva Leach

French traditional
arr. Carol Barratt

1. No - ël nou - ve - let, No - ël chan - tons i - ci. O__ bon - nes gens, chan -
   Sing now Christ is born, No - well sing_ we to - day. *O__ sing good folk, sing*
2. Or en Beth - lé - em, é - tant tous ré - u - nis, Trou - vent l'en - fant, le
   Now in Beth - le - hem, they in a__ sta - ble stay. *No__ crib for Him, now*
3. Et bien - tôt les Rois, par l'é - toile é - clair - cis, De l'O - ri - ent dont
   Rid - ing from the East, the Wise Men come to - day To__ Beth - le - hem, with

- tons tous à l'en - vi. Chan - tons No - ël pour l'en - fant nou - ve - let.
one and_ all I pray. *Sing we No - well, the Christ-child is new born.*
bœuf et_ l'âne aus - si. La crèche é - tait au lieu d'un ber - ce - let.
sleep-ing_ in the hay. *Ox - en and ass re - joice this hap-py morn.*
ils é - taient sor - tis, A Beth - lé - em vin - rent un ma - ti - net.
gifts they wend their way, Led by the star, which shines from dusk to dawn.

* This accompaniment can be used for whichever verse is performed as the final verse.

Disc 1

22 Piano accompaniment

23 Pronunciation guide

Omens of Spring

No. 2 from *Omens of Spring*

W. H. Anderson
(1882–1955)

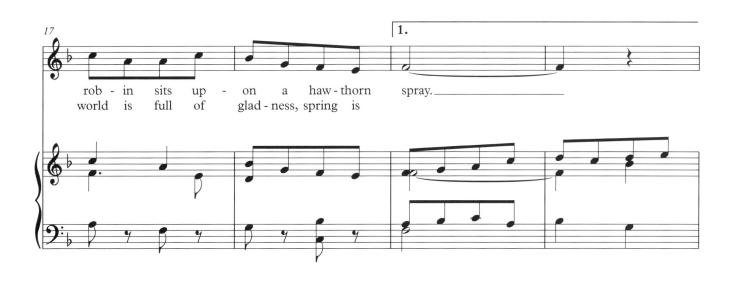

Disc 1

⑦ Piano accompaniment

⑧ Pronunciation guide

Die Nachtigall

The Nightingale

No. 2 from *Volks-Kinderlieder*

English words by
Elizabeth Eva Leach

German traditional
arr. Johannes Brahms
(1833–97)

Quem pastores laudavere

He whom shepherds laud with praises

English words by
Elizabeth Eva Leach

from Johann Hermann Schein's
Cantional (1627)

ed. Michael Pilkington

1. Quem pas-to-res lau-da-ve-re: Qui-bus An-ge-li dix-e-re:
   He whom shep-herds laud with prais-es While their flock near-by still gra-zes
2. Ad quem Re-ges am-bu-la-bant. Au-rum, Thus, Myr-rham por-ta-bant,
   He's the one three Kings make bold to, Frank-in-cense they bring and gold too

Ab-sit vo-bis jam ti-me-re, Na-tus est___ Rex glo-ri-ae.
For whom an-gels sing sweet phras-es He is born___ now, Christ the King!
Im-mo-la-bant haec sin-ce-re Le-o-ni___ vic-to-ri-ae.
Myrrh in pots with East-ern gla-zes Giv'n sin-cere-ly to___ the King.

3. Exultemus cum Maria,
   In caelesti Hierarchia,
   Natum promant voce pia,
   Dulci cum melodia.

3. *Let us with the Virgin sing now,*
   Make the highest heaven ring now,
   Telling of this wondrous thing now,
   Glory to the Lord bring now.

4. Christo Regi, Deo nato,
   Per Mariam nobis dato,
   Merito resonet vere:
   Laus honor et gloria.

4. *Christ the King, of God begotten,*
   Ours through Mary, ne'er forgotten,
   Sing we now in sweetest praises,
   And before the boy-king bow.

Disc 1

26 Piano accompaniment

27 Pronunciation guide

Song of the Boats

No. 2 from *Ten Ponder and William Songs*

Barbara Softly

Betty Roe
(born 1930)

Disc 1

28 Piano accompaniment

29 Pronunciation guide

for the children of Parkside School, Borehamwood

The Crocodile

Words and music by
Peter Jenkyns
(1921–96)

23
mp
They
f
mp
27
say he can live for a great ma - ny years With his croc - o - dile skin like an
30
ar - mour'd car. Be - cause of his teeth there is no - thing he fears; When he's
33
seen in a zoo you are saf - er by far.
f

Slower *ad lib.*

And now that my sto - ry is near - ly com-plete, Of the croc - o-dile's ha - bits I'm sure you might dream; But re - mem - ber, the on - ly one you'll chance to meet Is the liz-ard who lives on the banks of a stream.

colla voce

Tempo I

Disc 1

(30) Piano accompaniment

(32) Pronunciation guide

The Miller of Dee

English traditional

arr. Carol Barratt

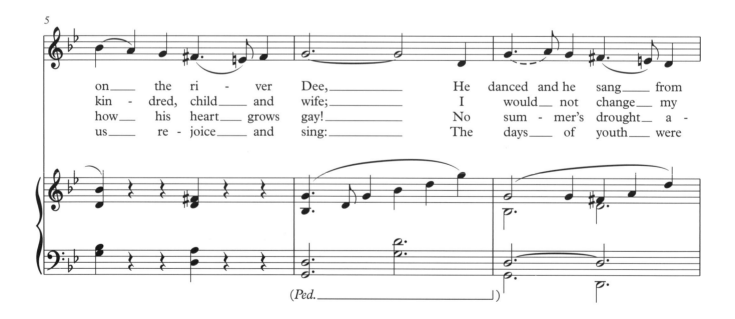

Disc 1
31 Piano accompaniment
32 Pronunciation guide

The Miller of Dee

English traditional

arr. Alan Bullard

wife;_____ I would not change my sta - tion for a - ny oth - er in
sing:_____ The days___ of youth were made for glee, and time_ is on___ the

life._____ No law - yer, sur-geon or doc - tor e'er had a groat from
wing._____ This song shall pass from me to thee, a - long this jo - vial

me._____ I care for no-bo-dy, no, not I, if no-bo-dy cares___ for
ring:_____ Let heart and voice___ and all a-gree to say___ 'long live___ the

1.   **last time**

me.'_____

king.'_____

Disc 1

35 Piano accompaniment

36 Pronunciation guide

Walking in the Air

Theme from *The Snowman*

Words and music by
Howard Blake
(born 1938)

AB 3128

Chil-dren gaze o-pen mouthed, ta-ken by sur - prise;

no-bo-dy down be-low be - lieves their eyes. We're

surf-ing in the air,_____ we're swim-ming in the fro - zen sky,_____

_ we're drift-ing o - ver i - cy moun-tains float-ing by._____

sleep; We're walk-ing in the air, we're
dan-cing in the mid - night sky, and ev-ery-one who sees us
greets us as we fly.

Disc 1

(33) Piano accompaniment

(34) Pronunciation guide

The Spinning Wheel

John Francis Waller
(1810–94)

Irish traditional

arr. Carol Barratt

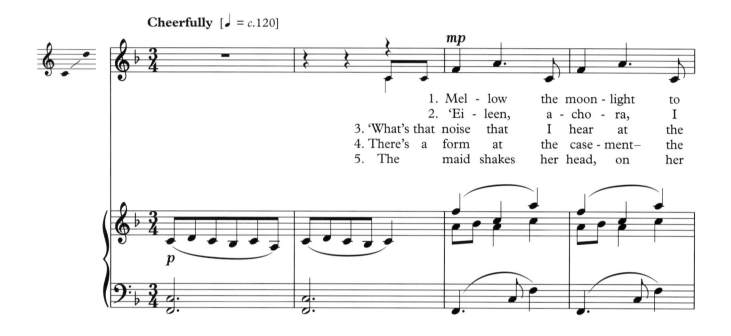

spin - ning; Bent o'er the fire, her blind grand - mo - ther,
flap - ping.' 'Ei - leen, I sure - ly hear some - bo - dy
un - der.' 'What makes you be shov - ing and mov - ing your
you, love; Get up on the stool, through the lat - tice step
lin - gers; A fright - en'd glance turns to her drow - sy grand -

sit - ting, Is croon - ing, and moan - ing, and drow - si - ly knit - ting:
sigh - ing.' ''Tis the sound mo - ther dear, of the sum - mer wind dy - ing.'
stool on, And sing - ing all wrong, that old song of "The Coo-lun"?'
light - ly, We'll rove in the grove while the moon's shin - ing bright - ly.'
- mo - ther, Puts one foot on the stool, spins the wheel with the oth - er.

CHORUS

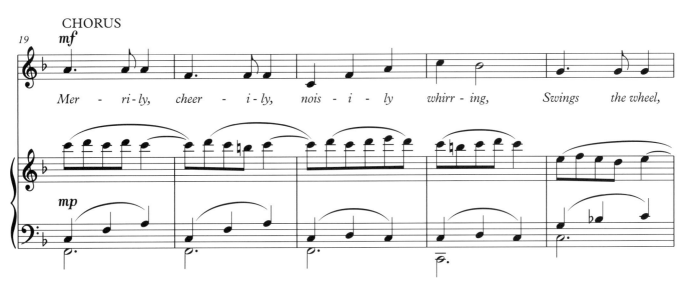

Mer - ri - ly, cheer - i - ly, nois - i - ly whirr - ing, Swings the wheel,

* This accompaniment can be used for whichever verse is performed as the final verse.

lat - tice a - bove her The maid steps– then leaps to the arms of her lov - er.

CHORUS

Slow - er– and slow - er– and slow - er the wheel swings; Low - er– and

low - er– and low - er the reel rings; Ere the reel and the wheel stopp'd their

ring - ing and mov - ing, Through the grove the young lov - ers by moon-light are rov - ing.

Disc 1

37 Piano accompaniment

38 Pronunciation guide

Where is love?

from *Oliver!*

Words and music by
Lionel Bart
(1930–99)

Slowly, but rhythmically [♩ = *c*.72]

Where_____ is love? Does it fall from skies a - bove?

Is it un-der-neath the wil - low tree_ that I've been dream - ing of?

Where_____ is she Who I close my eyes to see? Will I ev-er know the

Traditional Songs

Compiled by Lilija Zobens
and Leslie East

Compilers' note

One of the distinctive features of the ABRSM Singing syllabus is the requirement for candidates to offer an unaccompanied traditional song of their own choice. Full details are given in the syllabus booklet.

In *The ABRSM Songbook* series we have collected together some traditional songs suitable for this part of the Singing exam. Our collection has ranged widely, encompassing 26 countries. Our aim has been to extend the horizons of teachers and candidates, to take in songs from a variety of traditions, and to reflect in some part the origins of ABRSM examinees. We believe that candidates will enjoy the challenge of presenting a song from their own culture or, indeed, a song that comes from someone else's.

We have presented these songs here in a straightforward way. The main philosophy has been to encourage the singing of them in their original form and language. Then it has been the intention to tempt the singer into exploring and understanding the song from his or her own perspective. Explanations are given where thought necessary. Songs in English are in some cases accompanied by a brief explanation as to the song's meaning or origin where the words themselves are not explicit. Songs in other languages are given with their original language first and an English-singing version underneath or alongside. Either language could be used in an exam. In the case of Chinese and Greek songs, a transliteration of the original text is provided and the text is also given in the characters of the language. On the accompanying CD, each song can be heard pronounced in the original language. Even the English-language texts have been recorded, where possible in an appropriate accent.

When preparing one of these songs, it is important to experiment with the pitch to be used. Many traditional songs have extraordinarily wide ranges or very high or very low tessituras. Many in this collection have been notated at the pitch level used by the singer from whom the song was originally collected and recorded. Traditional singers always try to find a pitch level for a song that suits their own voices and singers using this collection should do the same.

Another area of freedom is in the interpretation of speed, dynamics and expression. Our collection gives only very brief guidance in this area or omits any guidance at all as traditional singers would be expected to develop their own distinctive interpretation of a song. The student should be encouraged to determine the way in which each of these songs might be sung through an understanding of the words, the meaning of the song and the musical character of the tune. Some songs have been notated with distinctive ornamentation but this shows merely a 'snapshot' of the song in one interpretation and candidates could ignore some or all of the ornamentation shown.

If one of these songs is chosen to be sung in an exam, then the student should ensure that its duration complies with the syllabus regulation shown. It is perfectly reasonable with traditional songs to make a selection of verses that make sense together, rather than sing the complete song.

Finally, it should be noted that the traditional songs gathered together here are NOT songs prescribed for ABRSM exams though obviously we hope they will be used for that purpose! They are intended as a resource for teachers and their students, to provide repertoire and an *approximate* guide to the standard of difficulty that might be appropriate to each grade. Sources of other traditional songs should be explored by teacher and student, especially songs from the student's own culture, or songs that show off a student's facility with another language. ABRSM examiners will welcome a rich variety of traditional songs when they examine singers in countries around the world.

Lilija Zobens and Leslie East

The collection of traditional songs was compiled by Lilija Zobens, with the assistance of Professor Jonathan Stock of Sheffield University. We are very grateful to Professor Stock for his contribution of songs from Malay, Chinese and Indonesian traditions to these anthologies. Notes on the origins and performance of the songs are by Lilija Zobens and Leslie East.

Disc 2

(1) Pronunciation guide

Aijā, žūžū

Go to sleep my little bear

Latvia

1. Ai - jā, žū - žū,   lā - ča bēr - nis,   ai - jā,   žū - žū,   pe - kai - nā - mi
Go   to sleep my   lit - tle bear, __   lul - la   -   by - by,   Feet as small as

kā - ji - ņā - mi,   žū - žū,   pe - kai - nā - mi   kā - ji - ņā - mi,   žū - žū.
ti - ny paws,   lul - la - by,   Feet as small as   ti - ny paws,   lul - la - by.

2. Tēvs aizgāja bišu kāpti, aijā, žūžū,
   Māte ogu palasīti, žūžū.

3. Tēvs atnesa medus podu, aijā, žūžū,
   Māte ogu vācelīti, žūžū.

4. Tie būs mazam bērniņami, aijā, žūžū,
   Par mierīgu gulēšanu, žūžū.

5. Kas vilkami, kas lāčami, aijā, žūžū,
   Mežā kāra šūpulīti, žūžū.

6. Lieli vīri izauguši, aijā, žūžū,
   Nešūpoti, neauklēti, žūžū.

2. *Daddy's gone to look for honey, lullaby-by,*
   Mummy's gone a-picking berries, lullaby.

3. *Daddy's brought a pot of honey, lullaby-by,*
   Mummy's filled a dish with berries, lullaby.

4. *You shall have them little baby, lullaby-by,*
   Close your eyes and slumber sweetly, lullaby.

5. *Brother wolf and brother bear, lullaby-by,*
   Sleep all night out in the air, lullaby.

6. *They grow up so strong and able, lullaby-by,*
   With no hand to rock their cradle, lullaby.

This must be the best-loved Latvian lullaby of all; every Latvian knows it! The Latvian homestead was never far away from the forest, which is where daddy and mummy go to gather the sweet berries and wild honey for their sleeping baby, who is likened to a bear-cub.

Keep this as simple and gentle as you dare, and very smooth.

Disc 2

② Pronunciation guide

Igama la Bantwana

Children's Song: Lullaby

South Africa (Zulu)

O tu - la, mntwa-na, O tu - la! Un - yo - ko a - ka -
O hush thee, ba - by, O hush____ thee! Thy moth - er is not

- mu - ko, U - se - le 'zin - ta - ben:____ U - hlu - shwa i - zi -
with thee, She tar - ried in the hills:____ The zig - zag trail hath

- gwe - gwe, I - wa!____ O tu - la, mntwa-na, O
held her, I - wa!____ O hush thee, ba - by, O

tu - la! Un - yo - ko u - se - zo - bu - ya, A -
hush____ thee! Thy moth - er soon is com - ing, She'll

- k'pa - te - le in - to en - hle, I - wa!____
bring thee pret - ty ber - ries, I - wa!____

A soothing song, sung to a baby whose mother has had to leave her child with another woman – perhaps to go to work.

Make it as gentle, smooth and rocking as you can. The asterisks mark where the intervals would be blurred in a downward glide (*portamento*). As this song would probably have been repeated over and over, try repeating it with some variations of dynamics and expression. 'Iwa' is a meaningless exclamation, possibly imitating the baby's cry.

Disc 2
3 Pronunciation guide

Jinkli Nona

Sinhalese girl

Malacca, Malaysia

CHORUS 1

Jin - kli No - na,   Jin - kli No - na   Yo ke - ray ka - zah,
Sinh - a - lese girl,   Sinh - a - lese girl,   o - pen up your door,

Ka - sa nun - teng   po - tra No - na   Kai lo - gu pa - sah?
Will you love me,   will you wed me,   though I may be poor?

CHORUS 2

Teng kan - tu   teng   Kan - tu teng fa - lah nun - teng,
I've no door and   I've   no roof but tell me what mat - ters more,

Fine (third time)

A - mor mi - nya   a - mor A - mor mi - nya kor - sang.
That we sleep with   stars a - bove us or that I'm yours?

1. O No - na mi - nya   No - na O No - na mi - nya kor - sang,
    Sinh - a - lese girl,   Sinh - a - lese girl, come and walk with me,

2. O No - na mi - nya   No - na Yo ta bai A - lor Ga - jah,
    Sinh - a - lese girl,   Sinh - a - lese girl, what is there to fear?

1. | **2.** back to Chorus 2

Ai No - na lah bem - fe - ta Ba - ba   ja kai na afe - sang.   - sang.
    I am wait - ing in your gar - den and I can - not sleep.   sleep.

Ke No - na teng kon - fian - sa Yo bi - ra lo - gu ka - sa.   - sa.
    Would you ra - ther live a - lone or know that I am here?   here?

This is one of the best-known Malaysian songs. It is the most famous 'branyo', a flirtatious social dance popular throughout the Portuguese settlements of south-west Malaysia. This version is in Kristang, a language spoken by fewer than 6,000 people of mixed Portuguese and Asian ancestry. Remember this is a dance song but try to introduce some variety of dynamics and characterization, perhaps in Chorus 2 and in any repeat.

ABRSM Publishing would like to thank Joan Marbeck and Don Beins for their help in researching this song.

Disc 2
(4) Pronunciation guide

Maple Sweet

Vermont, USA

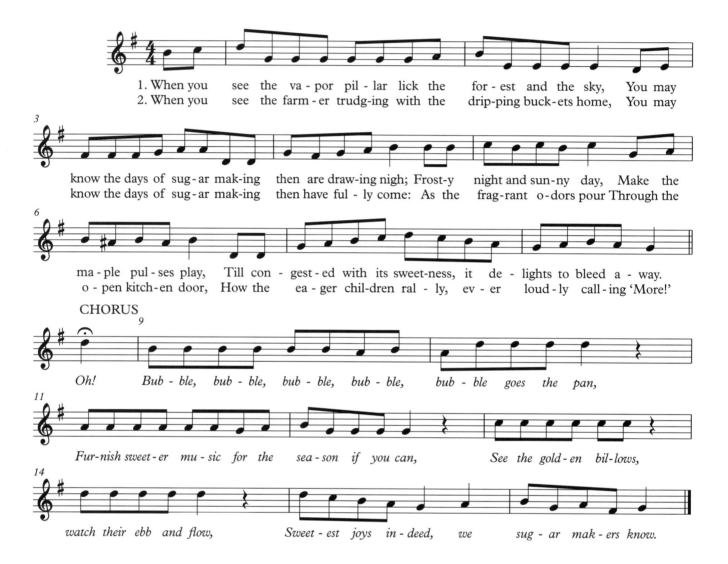

1. When you see the va-por pil-lar lick the for-est and the sky, You may
2. When you see the farm-er trudg-ing with the drip-ping buck-ets home, You may

know the days of sug-ar mak-ing then are draw-ing nigh; Frost-y night and sun-ny day, Make the
know the days of sug-ar mak-ing then have ful-ly come: As the frag-rant o-dors pour Through the

ma-ple pul-ses play, Till con-gest-ed with its sweet-ness, it de-lights to bleed a-way.
o-pen kitch-en door, How the ea-ger chil-dren ral-ly, ev-er loud-ly call-ing 'More!'

CHORUS

Oh! Bub-ble, bub-ble, bub-ble, bub-ble, bub-ble goes the pan,

Fur-nish sweet-er mu-sic for the sea-son if you can, See the gold-en bil-lows,

watch their ebb and flow, Sweet-est joys in-deed, we sug-ar mak-ers know.

3. Do you say you don't believe it?
   Take a saucer and a spoon,
   Though you're sourer than a lemon,
   you'll be sweeter very soon.
   Why, the greenest leaves you see,
   On the spreading maple tree,
   Though they sip and sip all summer
   will the autumn beauties be.

4. And for home or love,
   or any kind of sickness, 'tis the thing,
   Take in allopathic doses,
   and repeat it every spring;
   Until everyone you meet,
   If at home or on the street,
   Will be half a mind to bite you,
   for you look so very sweet.

Dating from the early 19th century, this song was collected in Underhill, Vermont, from the Jackson family, who have sung it for generations. When the warmer days of spring arrived, usually in March, maple trees were tapped and hung with buckets to catch their colourless sap, which flows freely after the cooler nights. For several weeks, men were busy tapping, gathering and boiling down the sap, making it into syrup and sugar.

Be careful not to make the quavers too regular or mechanical. Let the natural stresses of the words help shape your phrases. (Allopathic doses are regular medicines!)

Disc 2
(5) Pronunciation guide

Mick Miles

Verse words: Sussex, England
Tune and chorus words: Chris Bylett

There are lots of stories about the devil in Sussex, according to which Sussex folk delighted in tormenting him and outwitting him with native cunning. In this well-known tale, Mick Miles (or Mills) agreed to a race of a mile with the devil (we don't know why or how); the devil lost and Mick Miles kept his soul. From that time onwards, nothing has grown along the track of their race in St Leonard's Forest. The tune and words to the chorus are by singer and guitarist Chris Bylett, who lived on the edge of the forest.

A suggested tempo is ♩. = 68, to get a feel of the speed of the race.

Disc 2

 Pronunciation guide

Mr Colburn

St Croix, US Virgin Islands

1. Mis-tah Col-burn did-n't had no right to drive a-cross de la-goon-ah.
2. Mis-sis Col-burn, come hold de light; yo' hus-ban' hang on de go-bi tree.
3. All de t'ing wot bod-dah me, all gone in de la-goon mout'.

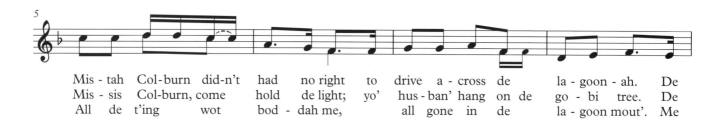

Mis-tah Col-burn did-n't had no right to drive a-cross de la-goon-ah. De
Mis-sis Col-burn, come hold de light; yo' hus-ban' hang on de go-bi tree. De
All de t'ing wot bod-dah me, all gone in de la-goon mout'. Me

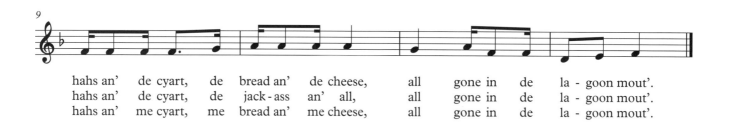

hahs an' de cyart, de bread an' de cheese, all gone in de la-goon mout'.
hahs an' de cyart, de jack-ass an' all, all gone in de la-goon mout'.
hahs an' me cyart, me bread an' me cheese, all gone in de la-goon mout'.

This song is based on a true incident about a man whose horse-drawn cart sank in the quicksand in a lagoon near Christiansted, St Croix. The jackass in verse 2 refers to the practice of hitching a second animal beside the horse in the stays of the cart.

Have fun trying to recreate the Caribbean dialect pronunciation here!

Disc 2

7   Pronunciation guide

Sing Ivy

Sussex, England

1. My fa - ther he gave me an a - cre of ground,
2. I ploughed it with a ram's horn, *Sing*
3. I sowed it with some pep - per corn,
4. I cut it with my pen - knife,

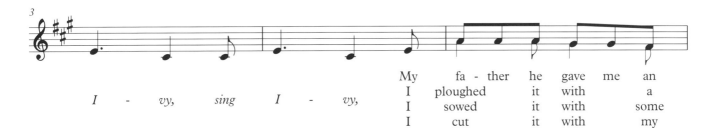

I - vy, sing I - vy,   My fa - ther he gave me an
                        I ploughed it with a
                        I sowed it with some
                        I cut it with my

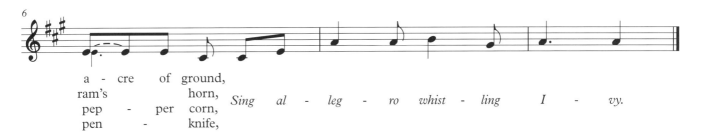

a - cre of ground,
ram's horn, *Sing al - leg - ro whist - ling I - vy.*
pep - per corn,
pen - knife,

5. I thrashed it with a rat's tail,
   Sing Ivy,…

6. I carried it away on a mouse's back,
   Sing Ivy,…

7. I measured it up by thimbleful,
   Sing Ivy,…

8. And money came back by sackfuls,
   Sing Ivy,…

This is a simpler version of an older ballad in which a supernatural knight sets a series of seemingly impossible tasks; here they are merely highly improbable! Take it at whatever speed is comfortable.

Disc 2

(8) Pronunciation guide

Spinn, spinn

Spin, spin

Germany

1. Spinn, spinn, mei-ne lie - be Toch - ter, ich kauf dir 'n Paar Schuh. Ja,
   Spin, spin, O my dear-est daugh-ter, I'll buy you some shoes. Yes,

ja, lie-be, lie - be Mut-ter, auch Schnal-len da - zu! Ich kann ja nicht spin-nen, es
yes, O my dear-est mo-ther, with buck - les one, two. I can - not spin, mo-ther, my

schmerzt mich mein Fin - ger Und tut und tut und tut mir so weh.
fin - ger does hurt me, It hurts and hurts and I can - not spin.

2. Spinn, spinn, meine liebe Tochter, ich kauf
   dir 'n Paar Strümpf.
   Ja, ja, liebe, liebe Mutter, auch Zwickeln
   darin!
   Ich kann ja nicht spinnen,…

3. Spinn, spinn, meine liebe Tochter, ich kauf
   dir ein Kleid.
   Ja, ja, liebe, liebe Mutter, nicht zu lang
   und nicht zu weit!
   Ich kann ja nicht spinnen,…

4. Spinn, spinn, meine liebe Tochter, ich kauf
   dir 'nen Mann.
   Ja, ja, liebe, liebe Mutter, dann streng ich
   mich an.
   Ich kann ja schon spinnen, es schmerzt
   mich kein Finger
   Und tut und tut und tut nicht mehr weh.

2. *Spin, spin, O my dearest daughter, I'll buy
   you some socks.
   Yes, yes, O my dearest mother, with fine
   'broidered clocks.
   I cannot spin,…*

3. *Spin, spin, O my dearest daughter, I'll buy
   you a gown.
   Yes, yes, O my dearest mother, with
   flounces all round.
   I cannot spin,…*

4. *Spin, spin, O my dearest daughter, I'll buy
   you a man.
   Yes, yes, O my dearest mother, as fast as
   I can.
   O now I am spinning, my finger is better.
   And now and now it hurts me no more.*

This is best sung strongly with almost a one-in-a-bar, dance-like feeling. Try to characterize the two voices.

AB 3128

Disc 2
(9) Pronunciation guide

Sus în poarta raiului

At the gates of Paradise

Romania

2. Şade Maica Domnului.
   Florile dalbe,...

3. C-un fiuţ micuţ în braţe.
   Florile dalbe,...

4. Fiul plînge, stare n-are.
   Florile dalbe,...

5. -Taci, fiule, nu mai plînge,
   Florile dalbe,...

6. Că m-oi duce, ţi-oi aduce
   Florile dalbe,...

7. Două mere, două pere,
   Florile dalbe,...

8. Toate patru aurele,
   Florile dalbe,...

9. Şi cheiţa de la rai,
   Florile dalbe,...

10. Să te faci mai mare crai.
    Florile dalbe,...

2. *There does sit the mother of Christ*
   Apple trees,...

3. *With her infant in her arms.*
   Apple trees,...

4. *He does cry and will not sleep.*
   Apple trees,...

5. *Hush, my child, and do not cry.*
   Apple trees,...

6. *I will go and bring to you*
   Apple trees,...

7. *Two fine apples, two fine pears;*
   Apple trees,...

8. *All the four of them in gold;*
   Apple trees,...

9. *And the key of Paradise.*
   Apple trees,...

10. *A great King you will become.*
    Apple trees,...

This is a *colinda*, or Christmas carol, probably best sung at a moderate speed.

Disc 2

(10) Pronunciation guide

Un jour sur le pont de Tréguier

One day upon the bridge in town

Brittany, France

1. Un jour sur le pont de Tré-guier, Lan-dé-ra, li-dé-ré, Un
One day up-on the bridge in town, Tra la la down dil - ly, One

-dé - ré, J'a - per - çus u - ne fil - le, Un deux trois
dil - ly, I saw a pret-ty young lass, One two three

dé - li - ra, Qui s'est mise à pleu-rer, Lan-dé-ra, li - dé - ré.____
fa la li, Tears pour-ing her face down, Tra la la down dil - ly.____

2. 'Ma fille, pourquoi donc pleurer?
   Landéra, lidéré.'
   'Je pleure après ma bague,
   Un deux trois délira,
   Que j'ai laissé tomber,
   Landéra, lidéré.'

3. 'Et que voudras tu me donner,
   Landéra, lidéré,
   Si je te la rapporte?
   Un deux trois délira.'
   'Je te donne un baiser,
   Landéra, lidéré.'

4. Au premier coup qu'il a plongé,
   Landéra, lidéré,
   Il voit l'anneau qui brille,
   Un deux trois délira,
   Au second l'a touché,
   Landéra, lidéré.

2. *'My child, please tell me why you weep,
   Tra la la down dilly.'
   'I've lost my diamond jewel,
   One two three fa la li,
   I've dropped it in the deep,
   Tra la la down dilly.'*

3. *'So what would you then give to me,
   Tra la la down dilly,
   If I returned it to you?
   One two three fa la li.'
   'I'd kiss you gratefully,
   Tra la la down dilly.'*

4. *At first when he dived in the flow,
   Tra la la down dilly,
   He saw the ring there shining,
   One two three fa la li,
   Touched it the second go,
   Tra la la down dilly.*

5. Pour le faire encore plonger,
   Landéra, lidéré,
   Elle fait un sourire,
   Un deux trois délira,
   Il n'a point remonté,
   Landéra, lidéré.

6. Le père en train de regarder,
   Landéra, lidéré,
   Etant à sa fenêtre,
   Un deux trois délira,
   Se met à sangloter,
   Landéra, lidéré.

7. 'J'avais trois garçons bien plantés,
   Landéra, lidéré,
   Et pour la même femme,
   Un deux trois délira,
   Tous trois se sont noyés,
   Landéra, lidéré!'

5. *A third dive she did him implore,*
   Tra la la down dilly,
   Smiling to goad him onward,
   One two three fa la li,
   He never surfaced more,
   Tra la la down dilly.

6. *And while the father watched the scene,*
   Tra la la down dilly,
   Out from his window leaning,
   One two three fa la li,
   Sobbing began to keen,
   Tra la la down dilly.

7. *'I've raised three young lads in this town,*
   Tra la la down dilly,
   And for the same young woman,
   One two three fa la li,
   All three I've now seen drown,
   Tra la la down dilly.'

On the surface, this appears to be a jolly song with its nonsense refrain. But it is actually a sad tale and, in the last three verses, needs subtle changes of character. Sing it at a moderate speed so that phrasing and articulation can be varied to help the characterization. In an exam, just the first three verses could be sung.

Disc 2

(11) Pronunciation guide

When the spring comes in

Sussex, England

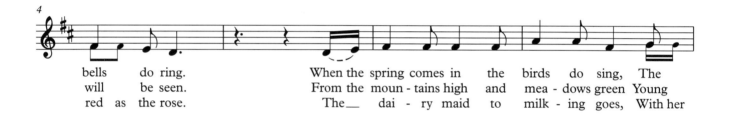

1. When the spring comes in the birds do sing, The lambs do play and the
2. From the moun - tains high and mea - dows green Young men and mai - dens
3. The__ dai - ry maid to milk - ing goes, With her bloom - ing cheeks as

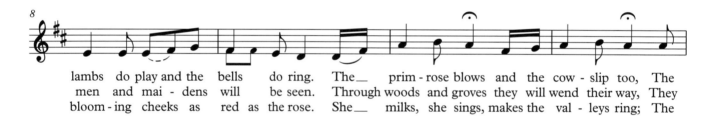

bells do ring. When the spring comes in the birds do sing, The
will be seen. From the moun - tains high and mea - dows green Young
red as the rose. The__ dai - ry maid to milk - ing goes, With her

lambs do play and the bells do ring. The__ prim - rose blows and the cow - slip too, The
men and mai - dens will be seen. Through woods and groves they will wend their way, They
bloom - ing cheeks as red as the rose. She__ milks, she sings, makes the val - leys ring; The

vio - lets in their sweet at - tire And the blue - bells shin - ing through the briar; The__
talk of tales and courts and sails, All lit - tle lambs a - round them play, And at
small birds on the bran - ches there Are list - 'ning to__ this love - ly fair, For she

daf - fo - dil - ly we all ad - mire While the dai - sies fade a - way.
night they on - ward bend their way, When the eve - ning star ap - pears.
is our mas - ter's trust and care, She is the plough - boy's joy.

Make the most of the lilting rhythm and the pauses in this song, but keep it simple and not too fast. Vary the dynamic in the repeat of the first line.

Disc 2

12 Pronunciation guide

小白菜
Xiao Baicai

Little Cabbage-face

Hebei Province, China

1. 小　　白　　菜　　（呀）　　　　地　　里＿＿＿　黄＿＿　（呀）；
   Xiao　Bai - cai　(ya)　　　di - li＿＿＿　huang＿　(ya);
   Xiao　Bai - cai　(ya),　　　small　and＿＿　pale＿＿　(ya);

三　　两　　岁　　上　　　没　　了　　娘＿＿＿　（呀）。
San　liang　sui　shang　　mei　le　niang＿＿　(ya).
On - ly　three,　I　　　lost　my　mo - ther.

亲　　娘＿＿＿　呀，　　　亲＿＿＿　娘＿＿＿　呀！
Qin - niang＿＿　ya,　　　Qin - niang＿＿　ya!
O　mo - ther,　　　dear＿＿　mo - ther!

2. 跟着爹爹还好过（呀）；
   只怕爹爹娶后娘（呀）。
   亲娘呀，亲娘呀！

3. 娶了后娘三年半（呀）；
   生个弟弟比我强（呀）。
   亲娘呀，亲娘呀！

2. Genzhe diedie hai hao guo (ya);
   Zhi pa diedie qu houniang (ya).
   Qinniang ya, Qinniang ya!

3. Qu le houniang san nian ban (ya);
   Sheng ge didi bi wo qiang (ya).
   Qinniang ya, Qinniang ya!

2. *Fine with Dad (ya), but so sad (ya)*
   When my Dad he found another.
   O mother, dear mother!

3. *Married her (ya), three years later,*
   They prefer my younger brother.
   O mother, dear mother!

This is a sad song which should thus be sung very slowly and softly. In this context, 'cabbage-face' is a term of affection.

AB 3128